I0365438

الوظيفة الكريمة

The Munificent LITANIES

a collection of supplications from the Qur'ān, sunnah and masters of the Qādirī path by

Imām Aḥmad Riḍā Khān رحمه الله

translation & footnotes by Yusuf Murray

Published in 2017 by
KUTUBIC
Birmingham, United Kingdom
www.kutubic.com

ISBN 978-1-9997720-1-7

Cover photographs: used under a Creative Commons Zero license
Executive Editor: Raza Alam
Translation, design & typesetting: Yusuf Murray

TRANSLITERATION KEY

CONSONANTS

ا	'	ز	z	ق	q
ب	b	س	s	ك	k
ت	t	ش	sh	ل	l
ث	th	ص	ṣ	م	m
ج	j	ض	ḍ	ن	n
ح	ḥ	ط	ṭ	ه	h
خ	kh	ظ	ẓ	و	w
د	d	ع	'	ى	y
ذ	dh	غ	gh	ة	h / t
ر	r	ف	f	ال	al-

VOWELS

Short

ـَ	a
ـِ	i
ـُ	u

Long

ـَا	ā
ـِي	ī
ـُو	ū

Doubled

ـِيّ	ī/iyy
ـُوّ	ū/uww

Dipthongs

ـَى	ay
ـَو	aw

الإهداء

I dedicate this translation to the soul of Ḥajī Muḥammad Yūsuf Francis ﵀. Born into a Roman Catholic family in 1903 in Trinidad & Tobago, he converted to Islam in 1925. Occupying his subsequent years with studies and struggles in the way of the Sunni-Sufi path, including a period of time spent with Shaykh ʻAbd al-ʻAlīm al-Ṣiddīqī ﵀, he contributed greatly to the propagation of Islam amongst the local population, through which many non-Muslims embraced Islam.

The translation of this work was completed whilst I was a guest of his descendants in Trinidad & Tobago. He passed away on April 17 1993 and rests in the main graveyard in St James, Port of Spain. The former Muslim president of the country buried at the foot of his grave, a lasting monument to the permanence of religious nobility over that of this mortal realm.

CONTENTS

Permission & Supplication.................................... III
Translator's Preface V
About The Author IX
Recite In The Morning & Evening 5
Recite In The Morning Only 24
After The Five Ritual Prayers 27
After The Morning & Afternoon Prayers 31
After The Morning Prayer 32
After The Evening Prayer 35
In The Night 35
After The Nighttime Prayer 36
Before Sleeping 40
Upon Rising From Sleep 42
The Night Vigil 42
The Remembrance Of The Four Strikes 43
Silent Remembrance 45
Inhalation & Exhalation 47
Envisaging One's Guide 47
Appendices 49
References.. 61
Bibliography... 65

PERMISSION & SUPPLICATION
by SHAYKH MANNĀN RIḌĀ KHĀN

I was filled with joy when I heard that Mawlānā Yusuf Murray has translated the wonderous work of Imām Aḥmad Riḍā Khān ﷺ, AL-WAẒĪFAT AL-KARĪMAH and others into English. In this work, my great-grandfather, our master Imām Aḥmad Riḍā Khān ﷺ has compiled such litanies and supplications that the one who regularly recites them will surely be blessed in both worlds. Not only is Mawlānā's mother-tongue English, but his Urdu is also eloquent and refined, leaving me in no doubt that this translation will be of great benefit and blessing to English-speaking Muslims.

With the blessings of the masters [*mashā'ikh*] of the Qādirī-Riḍawī path, I hereby grant permission to recite the Qur'ānic and Prophetic supplications contained within this work to every Sunni Muslim. I pray that Allah ﷻ grant this work the nobility of His acceptance, and place further blessings in the pen of Mawlānā Yusuf Murray that he may continue to serve the legacy of Imām Aḥmad Riḍā Khān ﷺ – *āmīn*!

(Shaykh) Mannān Riḍā Khān
Bareilly, India
14 Shawwāl 1438 AH / 8 July 2017 CE

TRANSLATOR'S PREFACE

This brief work penned by Imām Aḥmad Riḍā Khān ﷺ is a collection of supplications, litanies and spiritual exercises found in the Qur'ān, Prophetic tradition [*sunnah*] and the rituals of the masters of the Qādirī path. By implementing such recitations in one's daily life, an individual will find themselves closer to their Lord, distanced from sins and turmoils, and ultimately find inner tranquility, as the Qur'ān promises –

أَلَا بِذِكْرِ اللهِ تَطْمَئِنُّ الْقُلُوبُ

> *"Know: in the remembrance of Allah is the tranquility of hearts."* (13:28)

Most readers will be in no need of an introduction to the author-compiler, Imām Aḥmad Riḍā Khān ﷺ, but I wish to briefly draw the reader's attention to a point of interest in this collection. In these pages, the author mentions fifty-six litanies and spiritual exercises in total. Of these, forty-seven can be directly found in the same formula in the accepted collections of Prophetic tradition – with twenty of these being Qur'ānic supplications and the remainder Prophetic. Indeed, despite there being no intrinsic issue with such, only nine are litanies formulated after the Prophetic era.

This work, and the litanies it contains, therefore, are largely suitable and beneficial for recitation and implementation by one and all - whether they be aspirants[1] to the Qādirī path or not. It also reflects a tendency of the noble author to incline towards the pure Prophetic model in every aspect of his life. Indeed, his youngest son and heir, Shaykh Muṣṭafā Riḍā Khān ﷺ records him discussing this in AL-MALFŪẒ AL-SHARĪF,

> "My shelves are full of works of such (non-Prophetic) spiritual practices, but - all praise to Allāh ﷻ - I have never even considered them until this very day. I prefer to act upon those supplications which are mentioned in the Prophetic narrations. My trials have always been solved by means of them."[2]

This work has previously been translated and published by Mawlānā Kalīm al-Qādirī of Bolton, may Allāh ﷻ

---

1 The discussion of spiritual aspiration and allegiance is beyond the remit of this short preface. For an in-depth insight into this topic, the reader is advised to refer to "The Reality of Spiritual Allegiance [*Ḥaqīqat-i Bay'at*]" by Imām Aḥmad Riḍā Khān ﷺ and published by Kutubic (ISBN: 978-1-9997720-0-0).

2 Shaykh Muṣṭafā Riḍā Khān, *Al-Malfūẓ al-Sharīf* (Karachi: Maktaba tul Madina, 2011), p. 181.

reward him immensely. His work includes extensive beneficial footnotes and appendices but is printed in a larger size better suited to home study. No slight is intended to his splendid translation or plentiful talents by the publication of this edition, which is solely intended by means of its size to facilitate ease for those who recite these supplications on a daily basis.

In translating this work, I have relied upon the 2010 Urdu edition edited by Al-Madīnat al-'Ilmiyyah and printed by Maktaba Tul Madina (Karachi). With a view to maximising the readability of this text given its small trim size, I have included references for all of the litanies and exercises in the form of endnotes rather than footnotes, and only included essential explanatory comments as footnotes within the text.

I began the translation of this work on the morning of 25 Ramaḍān and completed it around the time of the night-vigil prayer on 27 Ramaḍān. The subsequent editing, typesetting and proofreading were commenced after Eid and completed on the birthdate of the Imām, 10 Shawwāl (1438 AH).

My guide and mentor, the scion of Imām Aḥmad Riḍā Khān ﵁, Shaykh Mannān Riḍā Khān kindly ennobled this work with his supplications and granted general permission [*ijāzah*] to the reader to recite the litanies and supplications contained herein through the chains of transmission of the luminaries of the Qādirī spiritual way.

As with all my works, I am forever indebted to Mawlānā Raza Alam (Burton Upon Trent, UK), Ali Hussain (Newport, UK) and Ayesha Ayaz (Birmingham, UK) for their diligent proof-reading and editing of the text, and, as always, my brother Hāfiẓ Faizur Rahman (New Delhi, India) for his unfailing assistance in deciphering complex Urdu / Persian phrasings and constructs. The reader is requested to join me in praying for their success and safety in both worlds, *āmīn*!

YUSUF MURRAY
Port of Spain, Trinidad & Tobago
The birthdate of Imām Aḥmad Riḍā Khān ﵀,
10 Shawwāl 1438 AH / 4 July 2017 CE

ABOUT THE AUTHOR

Imām Aḥmad Riḍā Khān ﷺ was born to a pious and scholarly family of Afghan descent on 10 Shawwāl 1272 AH (c. June 1865 CE) in the former princely city of Bareilly, situated in the modern-day state of Uttar Pradesh in India.

Beginning his studies according to the tradition at the tender age of four, he was fluent in Arabic by the age of six and qualified as jurist [*muftī*] when he was just shy of fourteen years of age. He immediately turned his attention to teaching the seekers of sacred knowledge and penning legal verdicts and other papers on a wide range of interests encompassing religious, social and material sciences.

At the age of twenty-two, he travelled the modest distance from Bareilly to the luminous town of Marehra, the spiritual epicentre of the offspring of the Messenger ﷺ in India, and pledged spiritual allegiance in the Qādirī path to Shāh Āl al-Rasūl al-Barakātī ﷺ. The *shaykh* was cognisant of the piety and erudition of the young Imām Aḥmad Riḍā Khān ﷺ to the extent that he immediately bestowed his viceregency [*khilāfah*] upon him, saying, "others come here to undertake spiritual development, but Aḥmad Riḍā has come developed".

He was particularly devoted to the blessed personage of the Messenger of Allah ﷺ, his kinsfolk and companions ؓ, and was defined by the deep and intuitive loyalty he felt to Imām Abū Ḥanīfah ؓ and Shaykh 'Abd al-Qādir al-Jīlānī ؓ. He afforded great honour and affection to the descendants of the Prophetic household, sitting them closest to him whilst hosting guests, presenting them with gifts and refusing to allow them to serve him in any way.

He was a personification of the Prophetic characteristic of balancing mercy with principle, embodying vast compassion and concern for people's wellbeing whilst never compromising on the principles set forth by the religion. Indeed, when schismatics reared their ugly head in the Indian subcontinent during his lifetime, he wrote extensive refutations of their heterodox excesses, with foresight that has since been vindicated many times over by the geopolitical upheavals brought about as a result of this sectarianism.

He performed two pilgrimages to the twin sanctuaries, in 1295 AH (1878 CE) and 1323 AH (1905 CE) and was proclaimed the 'reviver' [*mujaddid*] of the fourteenth century by the scholars of the Indian subcontinent and the Arabian Peninsula in 1318 AH (1900 CE) and 1321 AH (1906 CE) respectively.

Whilst remaining aloof from the vicissitudes of electoral politics, he was deeply troubled by the tribulations that befell both the Muslims of the subcontinent and the decline of the Ottoman Empire, supplicating for their preservation and offering his insightful counsel throughout his latter years.

His written works include a five-volume Arabic commentary of RADD AL-MUḤTĀR of Sayyid Ibn 'Ābidīn al-Shāmī ﵀, the first accurate translation of the Qur'ān in the Urdu language entitled KANZ AL-ĪMĀN and a twelve-volume collection of legal verdicts entitled AL-'AṬĀYĀ AL-NABAWIYYAH FĪ AL-FATĀWĀ AL-RIḌAWIYYAH. In total, he authored 679 works in his lifetime, writing an average of seventy pages a day throughout his adult life. Tragically, many of his works remain in manuscript form or have been lost to the passage of time.

He was also an accomplished poet, penning almost 150 compositions throughout his life in praise of the Divine

Majesty, the Prophetic being and the luminaries of the Muslim nation. His collected poems in the Urdu, Persian, Arabic and Hindi languages are published in a collection entitled ḤADĀ'IQ-I BAKHSHISH. Until today it is rare to find a religious gathering of Urdu-speaking Muslims anywhere in the globe except that a composition from his collection would be sung.

He continues to be the topic of much eulogistic and academic writing, with tens of biographies and PhD theses penned in English, Hindi and Urdu. In Arabic, the renowned Egyptian scholar Shaykh Khālid Thābit has authored a volume on his life and works entitled INṢĀF AL-IMĀM.

On 25 Ṣafar 1340 AH (c. October 1921 CE) he departed this temporal abode at the time of the Friday prayer as the caller to prayer cried out, "come to success."

YUSUF MURRAY
Bareilly, India
Ramaḍān 1436 AH / July 2015 CE

بِسۡمِ ٱللَّهِ ٱلرَّحۡمَٰنِ ٱلرَّحِيمِ

I praise the One who made supplication a form of worship - rather, the cerebrum of worship - and ordered His slaves, "supplicate to Me," and made binding His promise of acceptance, and whoever supplicated to his Lord, (He replies,) "I am present, My slave." Your Lord proclaims, "supplicate to me, I will accept it" and "when My servants ask you of Me, surely I am near, I answer the call of the supplicant when he calls unto Me." Verily, He is the All-Hearing and Accepting. And I invoke prayers and peace upon the one who reserved his accepted supplication for Day of Judgement, and upon his kinsfolk and companions, as long as rain pours from the sky, *āmīn.*

Praise[i] be to the Divine manifestations of generosity

---

i The introduction up to this point was penned by Imām Aḥmad Riḍā Khān ﷺ himself. The remainder was penned by his son, Shaykh Ḥāmid Riḍā Khān ﷺ, who comments, "Our illuminated master and sovereign (Imām Aḥmad Riḍā Khān ﷺ) wished to pen some words of introduction, yet these precious gems remained gathered as hidden pearls in his blessed breast. My heart did not permit me to remove even a single letter from the blessed phrases he had composed, thus they are presented in their ....

that gathered us as servants of the court of the liegelord of the universe, the greatest protecter, Muḥammad the Messenger of Allāh ﷺ. He who placed us in the generous protection of Shaykh 'Abd al-Qādir al-Jīlānī ؓ and cast upon us the merciful shade of the saints and masters of this way – in particular Imām Aḥmad Riḍā Khān ؓ – who informed us that our conscious Lord is conscientious of His slave raising his hands to Him and leaving empty-handed. He who ordered us to supplicate and guaranteed acceptance by means of His generosity, "supplication is binding upon you, for supplication averts fate, even after it has commenced."

This is a collection of those supplications, litanies and spiritual exercises from the court of the noble Messenger ﷺ transmitted to us at hands of our master Imām Aḥmad Riḍā Khān ؓ which were contained in a manuscript in the family collection. They are hereby presented for our brethren in faith and the aspirants of the Qādirī-Riḍawī way. We state with certainty that whoever recites and implements

---

.... original form up until this point. Thereafter, I have presented that which occurred to my modest understanding to the reader. Similarly, (Imām Aḥmad Riḍā Khān ؓ) did not entitle this book, thus I have added a chronological title and this foreword [*khuṭbah*]."

them shall be enriched with riches both worldly and religious and protected from every misfortune and tribulation. May the Lord benefit the entire *ahl al-sunnah* by means of their blessings - *āmīn, āmīn*!

The servant of the Qādirī-Riḍawī ménage,
Muḥammad Ḥāmid Riḍā Qādirī,
may Allāh forgive him.

RECITE IN THE MORNING & EVENING

From the passing of half the night[i] until the first rays of dawn is the morning. Whichever litanies are recited in this time will be considered as having being recited during the morning. Similarly, the evening is from the onset of the afternoon[ii] until sunset.

I

سُبْحَانَ اللّٰهِ وَبِحَمْدِهِ لَا قُوَّةَ إِلَّا بِاللّٰهِ مَا شَآءَ اللّٰهُ كَانَ وَمَا لَمْ يَشَأْ لَمْ يَكُنْ أَعْلَمُ أَنَّ اللّٰهَ عَلَى كُلِّ شَيْءٍ قَدِيرٌ وَأَنَّ اللّٰهَ قَدْ أَحَاطَ بِكُلِّ شَيْءٍ عِلْماً

subḥānallāhi wa bi-ḥamdihī lā quwwata illā bi-llāh. mā shā' allāhu kāna wa mā lam yasha' lam yakun. a'lamu anna-llāha 'alā kulli shay'in qadīr. wa anna-llāha qad aḥāṭa bi-kulli shay'in 'ilmā.

Glory be to Allāh with His praise. There is no power (to perform good deeds) save by

i To calculate this time, find the half-way point between the beginning times of *ṣalāt al-maghrib* and *ṣalāt al-fajr*.

ii From the beginning time of *ṣalāt al-ẓuhr*.

Allāh. Whatever Allāh willed came to be, and whatever He didn't will, didn't come to be. I know that Allāh has power over everything, and that verily Allāh's knowledge encompasses every thing.

Recite once.

II

The verse of the Throne [*āyat al-kursī*] once (see appendix 3), followed by reciting the following once,

حمٓ ۝١ تَنزِيلُ ٱلْكِتَـٰبِ مِنَ ٱللَّهِ ٱلْعَزِيزِ ٱلْعَلِيمِ
۝٢ غَافِرِ ٱلذَّنۢبِ وَقَابِلِ ٱلتَّوْبِ شَدِيدِ ٱلْعِقَابِ
ذِى ٱلطَّوْلِ ۖ لَآ إِلَـٰهَ إِلَّا هُوَ ۖ إِلَيْهِ ٱلْمَصِيرُ ۝٣

ḥā-mīm. tanzīl ul-kitābi minallāhi-l-'azīzi-l-'alīm. ghāfiri-dh-dhambi wa qābili-t-tawbi shadīdi-l-'iqāb dhi-ṭ-ṭawl. lā ilāha illā huwa ilayhi-l-maṣīr.

Ḥā Mīm. This Scripture is sent down from Allāh, the Almighty, the All-Knowing, Forgiver of sins and Accepter of repentance, Severe in punishment, Infinite in bounty. There is no god but Him; to Him is the ultimate return.[1]

III

The three '*qul*'-chapters [Sūrat al-Ikhlāṣ, Sūrat al-Falaq and Sūrat al-Nās] three times each. (See Appendix 6).

The three aforementioned litanies protect one from every tribulation: if they are read in the morning, then until the evening, and if read in the evening, until the morning.[2]

IV

بِسْمِ اللهِ مَا شَآءَ اللَّهُ لَا يَسُوقُ الْخَيْرَ إِلَّا اللهُ
مَا شَآءَ اللهُ لَا يَصْرِفُ السُّوْءَ إِلَّا اللَّهُ مَا شَآءَ
اللهُ مَا كَانَ مِنْ نِّعْمَةٍ فَمِنْ اللهِ مَا شَآءَاللهُ لَا
حَوْلَ وَلَا قُوَّةَ إِلَّا بِا اللهِ

bismillāhi mā shā' allāhu lā yasūqu-l-khayra illa-llāh. mā shā' allāhu lā yaṣrifu-s-ū'a illa-llāh. mā shā' allāhu mā kāna min-ni'matin famin allāh. mā shā' allāhu lā ḥawla wa lā quwwata illā bi-llāh.

In the name of Allāh. As Allāh willed: there is no manifestation of good except from Allāh.

As Allāh willed: there is no averting of evil except from Allāh. As Allāh willed: all that manifests from bestowals is from Allāh. As Allāh willed: there is no power nor might save by Allāh.

This grants the reciter protection from seven things: burning, drowning, theft, snakes, scorpions, Satan and the ruler.[3]

V

أَعُوْذُ بِكَلِمَاتِ اللهِ التَّآمَّاتِ مِنْ شَرِّ مَا خَلَقَ

a'ūdhu bi-kalimāti-llāhi-t-tāmmāti min sharri mā khalaq.

I seek refuge in the complete words of Allāh from the evil of that which He created.

Recite three times. This grants the reciter protection from poisonous animals such as snakes and scorpions.[4]

VI

بِسْمِ اللَّهِ الَّذِى لَا يَضُرُّ مَعَ اسْمِهِ شَىْءٌ فِى الْاَرْضِ وَلَا فِى السَّمَآءِ وَهُوَ السَّمِيعُ الْعَلِيْم

bismillāhi-l-ladhī lā yaḍurru ma'a-smihī shayun fi-l-arḍi wa lā fi-s-samā'i wa huwa-s-samī'u-l-'alīm.

In the name of Allāh, with Whose name nothing in the heaven or earth can harm, and He is the All-Hearing, All-Knowing.[5]

Recite three times for protection from poison and harm.

VII

رَضِيْتُ بِاللهِ رَبًّا وَّبِالْإِسْلَامِ دِيْنًا وَّبِسَيِّدِنَا وَمَولَانَا مُحَمَّدٍ صَلَّى اللهُ عَلَيْهِ وَسَلَّم نَبِيًّا وَّ رَسُوْلًا

raḍītu bi-llāhi rabbā. wa bi-l-islāmi dīnā. wa bi-sayyidinā wa mawlānā muḥammadin ṣalla-llāhu 'alayhi wa sallama nabiyya-w-wa rasūlā.

I am pleased with Allāh as a Lord, Islam as a religion and our liege lord and master Muhammad ﷺ as a Prophet and Messenger.

Recite three times: come the Day of Judgement, Allāh will - by His generosity - please the one who recites this litany.[6]

VIII

حَسْبِيَ اللَّهُ لَا إِلَٰهَ إِلَّا هُوَ ۖ عَلَيْهِ تَوَكَّلْتُ ۖ وَهُوَ
رَبُّ الْعَرْشِ الْعَظِيمِ

ḥasbiya-llāhu lā ilāha illā hū. 'alayhi tawakkaltu wa huwa rabbu-l-'arshi-l-'aẓīm.

Allāh suffices me – there is no god but He. I have placed my trust in Him. He is the Lord of the majestic throne.

Recite ten times for protection from every tribulation and mischief. The narration [*hadīth*] mentions seven times[7], and ten times has been reported from our master, Shaykh 'Abd al-Qādir ﵁. This servant [*faqīr*] acts upon this, and – all praise to Allāh ﷻ – has found it to suffice every intent.

IX

فَسُبْحَٰنَ ٱللَّهِ حِينَ تُمْسُونَ وَحِينَ تُصْبِحُونَ
﴿١٧﴾ وَلَهُ ٱلْحَمْدُ فِى ٱلسَّمَٰوَٰتِ وَٱلْأَرْضِ وَعَشِيًّا
وَحِينَ تُظْهِرُونَ ﴿١٨﴾ يُخْرِجُ ٱلْحَىَّ مِنَ ٱلْمَيِّتِ
وَيُخْرِجُ ٱلْمَيِّتَ مِنَ ٱلْحَيِّ وَيُحْيِ ٱلْأَرْضَ بَعْدَ

مَوْتِهَاۚ وَكَذَٰلِكَ تُخْرَجُونَ ﴿١٩﴾

fa-subḥāna-llāhi ḥīna tumsūna wa ḥīna tuṣbiḥūn. wa lahu-l-ḥamdu fi-s-samāwāti wa-l-arḍi wa 'ashiyya-w-wa ḥīna tuẓhirūn. yukhriju-l-ḥayya mina-l-mayyiti wa yukhriju-l-mayyita mina-l-ḥayyi wa yuḥyi-l-arḍa ba'da mawtihā wa ka-dhālikha tukhrajūn.

So glorify Allāh when you reach the evening and when you reach the morning. All praise is His in the heavens and the earth - in the late afternoon, and at midday. He brings the living from the dead and brings the dead from the living and brings to life the earth after its lifelessness. And so too you will be brought out.

Recite once. If an individual is unable to recite any litanies on a given day, this alone will suffice. Furthermore, it compensates for the losses sustained in any given day and night.[8]

X

أَفَحَسِبْتُمْ أَنَّمَا خَلَقْنَٰكُمْ عَبَثًا وَأَنَّكُمْ إِلَيْنَا

لَا تُرْجَعُونَ ﴿١١٥﴾ فَتَعَٰلَى ٱللَّهُ ٱلْمَلِكُ ٱلْحَقُّ ۖ لَآ إِلَٰهَ
إِلَّا هُوَ رَبُّ ٱلْعَرْشِ ٱلْكَرِيمِ ﴿١١٦﴾ وَمَن يَدْعُ مَعَ
ٱللَّهِ إِلَٰهًا ءَاخَرَ لَا بُرْهَٰنَ لَهُۥ بِهِۦ فَإِنَّمَا حِسَابُهُۥ
عِندَ رَبِّهِۦٓ ۚ إِنَّهُۥ لَا يُفْلِحُ ٱلْكَٰفِرُونَ ﴿١١٧﴾ وَقُل رَّبِّ
ٱغْفِرْ وَٱرْحَمْ وَأَنتَ خَيْرُ ٱلرَّٰحِمِينَ ﴿١١٨﴾

afaḥasibtum annamā khalaqnākum 'abatha-w-wa annakum ilaynā lā turja'ūn. fata'āla-llāhu-l-maliku-l-ḥaqqu lā ilāha illā huwa rabbu-l-'arshi-l-karīm. wa may-yad'u ma'a-llāhi ilāhan 'ākhara lā burhāna lahū bihī fa'innamā ḥisābuhū 'inda rabbih. innahū lā yufliḥu-l-kafirūn. wa qu-r-rabbi-ghfir wa-rḥam wa anta khayru-r-raḥimīn.

Did you think We had created you aimlessly, and that you would not return to Us? Exalted is Allāh, the true King, there is no god but Him, the Lord of the Glorious Throne! Whoever prays alongside Allāh to another god - for whose existence he has no evidence - will face his reckoning with his Lord. The disbelievers will not attain salvation. Submit, "my Lord, forgive and have mercy: You are the most merciful of all."[9]

Recite once for protection from Satan and evil spirits [*jinn*].

XI

أَعُوْذُ بِاللّٰهِ السَّمِيْعِ الْعَلِيْمِ مِنَ الشَّيْطَانِ الرَّجِيْمِ

aʿūdhu bi-llāhi-s-samīʿi-l-ʿalīmi mina-sh-shayṭāni-r-rajīm.

I seek refuge in Allāh – the All-Hearing, the All-Knowing – from the accursed Satan.

Recite three times, followed by the last three verses of Sūrat al-Ḥashr once:

هُوَ ٱللَّهُ ٱلَّذِى لَآ إِلَٰهَ إِلَّا هُوَ ۖ عَٰلِمُ ٱلْغَيْبِ
وَٱلشَّهَٰدَةِ ۖ هُوَ ٱلرَّحْمَٰنُ ٱلرَّحِيمُ ﴿٢٢﴾ هُوَ ٱللَّهُ ٱلَّذِى
لَآ إِلَٰهَ إِلَّا هُوَ ٱلْمَلِكُ ٱلْقُدُّوسُ ٱلسَّلَٰمُ ٱلْمُؤْمِنُ
ٱلْمُهَيْمِنُ ٱلْعَزِيزُ ٱلْجَبَّارُ ٱلْمُتَكَبِّرُ ۚ سُبْحَٰنَ ٱللَّهِ
عَمَّا يُشْرِكُونَ ﴿٢٣﴾ هُوَ ٱللَّهُ ٱلْخَٰلِقُ ٱلْبَارِئُ
ٱلْمُصَوِّرُ ۖ لَهُ ٱلْأَسْمَآءُ ٱلْحُسْنَىٰ ۚ يُسَبِّحُ لَهُۥ مَا فِى
ٱلسَّمَٰوَٰتِ وَٱلْأَرْضِ ۖ وَهُوَ ٱلْعَزِيزُ ٱلْحَكِيمُ ﴿٢٤﴾

huwa-llāhu-l-ladhī lā ilāha illā hū. 'ālimu-l-ghaybi wa-sh-shahādati huwa-r-raḥmānu-r-raḥīm. huwa-llāhu-l-ladhī lā ilāha illā hū. al-maliku-l-quddūsu-s-salāmu-l-mu'minu-l-muhayminu-l-'azīzu-l-jabbāru-l-mutakabbir. subḥāna-llāhi 'ammā yushrikūn. huwa-llāhu-l-khāliqu-l-bāri'u-l-muṣawwiru lahu-l-asmā'u-l-ḥusnā. yusabbiḥu lahū mā fi-s-samāwāti wa-l-arḍ. wa huwa-l-'azīzu-l-ḥakīm.

He is Allāh: there is no god other than Him: the Knower of all that is unseen and seen, He is the Most Compassionate, the Most Merciful. He is Allāh, other than whom there is no god, the Sovereign, the Most-Pure, the Giver of peace, the Bestower of Faith, the Protector, the Exalted, the Mighty, the Superior. Glorified is Allāh above whatever they associate with Him. He is Allāh: the Creator, the Originator, the Shaper. The best names belong to Him. Everything in the heavens and earth glorifies Him: He is the Almighty, the Wise.

If an individual recites this in the day, seventy thousand angels shall supplicate for their forgiveness until night, and if an individual passes away on that day, they will be a martyr [*shahīd*], and the same is true for the one who recites it by night until the following day.[10]

XII

اَللّٰهُمَّ اِنَّا نَعُوْذُ بِكَ مِنْ اَنْ نُشْرِكَ بِكَ شَيْئًا نَعْلَمُهٗ وَنَسْتَغْفِرُكَ لِمَا لَا نَعْلَمُهٗ

allāhumma innā na'ūdhu bika min an nushrika bika shay'an na'lamuhū wa nastaghfiruka limā lā na'lamuh.

O' Allāh! We seek refuge with You from associating anything with You knowingly, and we seek Your forgiveness from that of which we are unknowing.[11]

Recite three times, one will die upon faith [*īmān*].

XIII

بِسْمِ اللهِ عَلٰى دِيْنِيْ بِسْمِ اللهِ عَلٰى نَفسِىْ وَ وُلْدِىْ وَ اَهْلِىْ وَ مَالِىْ

bismillāhi 'alā dīnī bismillāhi 'alā nafsī wa wuldī wa ahlī wa mālī.

(I invoke) the name of Allāh upon my religion, the name of Allāh upon my soul, my offspring, my family and my wealth.

Recite three times for the protection of one's religion, faith, life, wealth and offspring.[12]

XIV

اَللَّهُمَّ مَا اَصْبَحَ لِي مِنْ نِعْمَةٍ اَوْ بِاَحَدٍ مِنْ خَلْقِكَ فَمِنْكَ وَحْدَكَ لَا شَرِيْكَ لَكَ فَلَكَ الْحَمْدُ وَلَكَ الشُّكْرُ

allāhumma mā aṣbaḥa lī min-ni'matin aw bi-aḥadi-m-min khalqik. faminka waḥdaka lā sharīk lak. falaka-l-ḥamdu wa laka-sh-shukr.

O' Allāh, whatever blessings I or any of your creation begin this day with, they are from You. You are One, You have no partners. For You is all praise and for You is all gratitude.

Reciting this in the morning is expressing gratitude for the blessings of that day, whilst reciting it in the evening is for those of that night.[13] In the evening, replace the word أَصْبَحَ [*aṣbaḥa*] with أَمْسَى [*amsā*].

This servant also adds the following recitation afterwards,

لَا إِلٰهَ إِلَّا أَنْتَ سُبْحٰنَكَ إِنِّي كُنْتُ مِنَ الظّٰلِمِيْنَ

lā ilāha illā anta subḥānaka innī kuntu mina-ẓ-ẓālimīn.

There is no god but You, Glory be to You. Indeed I have been of the wrongdoers.

XV

بِسْمِ اللهِ جَلِيْلِ الشَّأْنِ عَظِيْمِ الْبُرْهَانِ شَدِيْدِ السُّلْطَانِ مَا شَآءَ اللهُ كَانَ أَعُوْذُ بِاللهِ مِنَ الشَّيْطٰنِ الرَّجِيْمِ

bismillāhi jalīli-sh-sha'ni aẓīmi-l-burhāni shadīdi-s-sulṭān. mā shā' allāhu kāna a'ūdhu bi-llāhi mina-sh-shayṭāni-r-rajīm.

In the name of Allāh: Majestic in rank, Magnificent in Proof, the All-Powerful Ruler. Whatever Allāh willed came to pass. I seek refuge with Allāh from the accursed Satan.

Recite once for protection from Satan and his armies.[14]

XVI

اَللّٰهُمَّ اِنِّي اَصْبَحْتُ اُشْهِدُكَ وَاُشْهِدُ حَمَلَةَ عَرْشِكَ وَمَلٰٓئِكَتَكَ وَجَمِيعَ خَلْقِكَ أَنَّكَ أَنْتَ اللّٰهُ لَا إِلَهَ إِلَّا أَنْتَ وَأَنَّ مُحَمَّدًا عَبْدُكَ وَرَسُولُكَ صَلَّى اللهُ تَعَالٰى عَلَيْهِ وَسَلَّمَ

allāhumma innī aṣbaḥtu ushhiduka wa ushhidu ḥamalata 'arshika wa malā'ikataka wa jamī'a khalqik. annaka anta-llāhu lā ilāha illā anta wa anna muḥammadan 'abduka wa rasūluka ṣalla-llāhu ta'ālā 'alayhi wa sallam.

O' Allāh, I have reached the morning making You a witness, and making those a witness who carry Your Throne and Your angels and all of Your creation that verily You are Allāh: there is no god but you, and that Muḥammad is Your Bondsman and Messenger, prayers and peace of Allāh Almighty upon him.

Recite four times, each recitation will free each of the four parts of the body from the fire of hell.[15]

XVII

اَللّٰهُمَّ لَكَ الْحَمْدُ حَمْدًا دَائِماً مَّعَ دَوَامِكَ وَلَكَ الْحَمْدُ حَمْدًا خَالِدًا مَّعَ خُلُوْدِكَ وَلَكَ الْحَمْدُ حَمْدًا لَّا مُنْتَهٰى لَهٗ دُوْنَ مَشِيْئَتِكَ وَلَكَ الْحَمْدُ حَمْدًا عِنْدَ كُلِّ طَرْفَةِ عَيْنٍ وَّتَنَفُّسِ كُلِّ نَفْسٍ

allāhumma laka-l-ḥamdu ḥamdan dā'ima-m-ma'a dawāmik. wa laka-l-ḥamdu ḥamdan khālida-m-ma'a khulūdik. wa laka-l-ḥamdu ḥamda-l-lā muntahā lahū dūna mashī'atik. wa laka-l-ḥamdu ḥamdan 'inda kulli ṭarfati 'ayni-w-wa tanaffusi kulli nafs.

O' Allāh! For you is all Praise: an eternal praise with Your eternity. For You is all praise: a perpetual praise with Your perpetuity. For You is all praise: a praise that has no limits save Your divine will. For You is all praise: praise in every moment and upon the breath of every being.

Recite once, it will be as though the reciter fulfilled the rights of worship in that day and night.[16]

XVIII

اَللّٰهُمَّ اِنِّي اَعُوْذُ بِكَ مِنَ الْهَمِّ وَالْحُزْنِ وَاَعُوْذُ بِكَ مِنَ الْعَجْزِ وَالْكَسَلِ وَاَعُوْذُ بِكَ مِنَ الْجُبْنِ وَالْبُخْلِ وَاَعُوْذُ بِكَ مِنْ غَلَبَةِ الدَّيْنِ وَقَهْرِ الرِّجَالِ

allāhumma innī a'ūdhu bika mina-l-hammi wa-l-ḥuzn. wa a'ūdhu bika mina-l-'ajzi wa-l-kasal. wa a'ūdhu bika mina-l-jubni wa-l-bukhl. wa a'ūdhu bika min ghalabati-d-dayni wa qahri-r-rijāl.

O' Allāh! I seek refuge with You from sorrow and grief. I seek refuge with You from inability and laziness. And I seek refuge with you from cowardice and miserliness. And I seek refuge with you from being overcome by debts and the force of men.

Recite once to be free from sorrows and grief. For the payment of debts, recite eleven times.[17]

IXX

يَا حَيُّ يَا قَيُّوْمُ بِرَحْمَتِكَ اَسْتَغِيْثُ فَلَا تَكِلْنِيْ

إِلَىٰ نَفْسِيْ طَرْفَةَ عَيْنٍ وَّأَصْلِحْ لِيْ شَأْنِيْ كُلَّهُ

yā ḥayyu yā qayyūmu bi-raḥmatika astaghīth. fa-lā takilnī ilā nafsī ṭarfata ʿayni-w-wa aṣliḥ lī shaʾnī kullah.

O' Ever-Living, O' Eternal! I beseech by Your mercy, do not make me subservient to my ego for even a moment, and rectify all my affairs for me.

Recite once, all of one's tasks will be accomplished.

XX

اَللّٰهُمَّ خِرْلِيْ وَاخْتَرْلِيْ وَلَاتَكِلْنِيْ إِلَى اخْتِيَارِيْ

allāhumma khirlī wa-khtarlī wa lā takilnī ila-khtiyārī.

O' Allāh, make it beneficial for me, and chose for me, and do not make me enslaved to my desires.

Recite seven times, this will be a source of goodness [*istikhārah*] for the tasks of the day and night.[18]

XXI

Recite the master of prayers for forgiveness [*sayyid al-istighfār*] once or thrice. One's sins will be forgiven, and if they die during that day or night, they will be considered a martyr.

اَللّٰهُمَّ اَنْتَ رَبِّي لَا اِلٰهَ اِلَّا اَنْتَ خَلَقْتَنِيْ وَاَنَا عَبْدُكَ وَاَنَا عَلٰى عَهْدِكَ وَوَعْدِكَ مَا اسْتَطَعْتُ اَعُوْذُ بِكَ مِنْ شَرِّ مَا صَنَعْتُ أَبُوْءُ لَكَ بِنِعْمَتِكَ عَلَيَّ وَأَبُوْءُ لَكَ بِذَنْبِيْ فَاغْفِرْ لِي فَاِنَّهُ لَا يَغْفِرُ الذُّنُوْبَ اِلَّا اَنْتَ

allāhumma anta rabbī lā ilāha illā ant. khalaqtanī wa ana 'abduka wa ana 'alā 'ahdika wa wa'dika ma-staṭa't. a'ūdhu bika min sharri mā ṣana'tu abū'u laka bi-ni'matika 'alayya wa abū'u laka bi-dhambī. fa-ghfir lī fa-innahū lā yaghfiru-dh-dhunūba illā ant.

O' Allāh! You are my Lord: there is no god but You. You created me and I am Your slave. I am upon Your covenant and promise to the best of my ability. I seek your refuge from the evil I have committed. I accept Your bestowals upon me and I accept my sins. So forgive me: for verily there is no forgiver of sins save You![19]

This servant adds the following to this recitation, and finds that whichever task carries a risk of harm, the Lord protects me from it:

وَاغْفِرْ لِكُلِّ مُؤْمِنٍ وَّ مُؤمِنَةٍ

wa-ghfir li-kulli mu'mini-w-wa mu'minah.

And forgive every believing man and woman.

XXII

لَا اِلٰهَ اِلَّا اللهُ الْمَلِكُ الْحَقُّ الْمُبِيْنُ

lā ilāha illa-llāhu-l-maliku-l-ḥaqqu-l-mubīn.

There is no god but Allāh: the True and Manifest King.

Recite one hundred times: one will never be destitute in this world, nor lonely in the grave nor fearful come Resurrection.[20]

I

بِسْمِ اللهِ الرَّحْمٰنِ الرَّحِيْمِ وَلَا حَوْلَ وَلَا قُوَّةَ إِلَّا بِاللهِ الْعَلِيِّ الْعَظِيْمِ

bismillāhi-r-raḥmāni-r-raḥīm. wa lā ḥawla wa lā quwwata illā bi-llāhi-l-'aliyyi-l-'aẓīm.

In the name of Allāh: the Compassionate, the Most-Merciful. There is no power or might save with Allāh: the Most-High, the Majestic.

Every task will be accomplished and one will remain protected from Satan.[i]

II

Recite Sūrat al-Ikhlāṣ (see Appendix 6.1) eleven times: if Satan and his entire army try to coerce an individual (who has recited this litany) to commit a sin, they will be unable to do so until the individual does so voluntarily.[21]

i Some prints of this work state that this is to be read eleven times whereas others do not specify an amount.

III

يَا حَيُّ يَا قَيُّوْمُ لَا اِلٰهَ اِلَّا اَنْتَ

yā ḥayyu yā qayyūmu lā ilāha illā ant.

O' Ever-Living, O' Ever-Lasting: there is no god but You!

Recite forty-one times, one's heart will become alive and they will die upon faith [*īmān*].

IV

سُبْحَانَ اللهِ الْعَظِيْمِ وَبِحَمْدِهٖ

subḥāna-llāhi-l-'aẓīmi wa bi-ḥamdih.

Glory be to Allāh, the Magnificent: and praise be to Him.

Recite three times: one will remain safe from madness, leprosy and blindness.[22]

V

Recite at least one part [*juz*] of the noble Qur'ān: if possible before sunrise. If the sun begins to rise, pause and engage in other litanies until the sun has fully risen. It is disliked [*makrūh*] to recite the Qur'ān in those three times in which performing ritual prayer [*ṣalāh*] is impermissible.[i]

VI

Recite one section [*ḥizb*] of Dalā'il al-Khayrāt.

VII

Recite one's chain of spiritual succession [*shajarah*].[ii]

NOTE: The recitation of Dalā'il al-Khayrāt and one's chain of spiritual succession can be completed before or after sunrise.

---

i There are three such times: (1) immediately after sunrise for a period of approximately twenty minutes, (2) when the sun is at its zenith, and (3) immediately before sunset for a period of approximately twenty minutes.

ii One's chain of spiritual succession [*shajarah*] details the lineage of teachers and guides connecting them to the Messenger ﷺ. Varying branches of spiritual lineage have different presentations of this chain in the form of poetry and supplications. If one has pledged allegiance in any spiritual chain, they should recite it at this time as mentioned by the author.

AFTER THE FIVE RITUAL PRAYERS

I

Recite the verse of the throne [*āyat al-kursī*] (see Appendix 3) once: one will enter Paradise [*jannah*] as soon as they die.[23]

II

أَسْتَغْفِرُ اللهَ الَّذِىْ لَا اِلٰهَ اِلَّا هُوَ الْحَىُّ الْقَيُّوْمُ وَاَتُوْبُ اِلَيْهِ

astaghfiru-llāha-l-ladhī lā ilāha illā huwa-l-ḥayyu-l-qayyūmu wa atūbu ilayh.

I seek forgiveness from Allāh: there is no god but He. He is the Ever-Living, the Ever-Lasting, and I repent to Him.

Recite three times: one's sins will be forgiven even if they are equal to the foam on the oceans.[24]

III

Recite the litany [*tasbīḥ*] of Lady Fāṭimah ﷺ:

سُبْحَانَ اللهِ	*subḥāna-llāh*	Glory be to Allāh

Thirty-three times,

اَلْحَمْدُ لِلّٰهِ	*al-ḥamdu li-llāh*	All praise is for Allāh

Thirty-three times,

اَللهُ اَكْبَرُ	*allāhu akbar*	Allāh is the Greatest

Thirty-four times,

Followed by,

لَا اِلٰهَ اِلَّا اللّٰهُ وَحْدَهٗ لَا شَرِيْكَ لَهٗ لَهُ الْمُلْكُ وَلَهُ الْحَمْدُ وَهُوَ عَلٰى كُلِّ شَيْءٍ قَدِيْرٌ

lā ilāha illa-llāhu waḥdahū lā sharīka lah. lahu-l-mulku wa lahu-l-ḥamd. wa huwa ʿalā kulli shay'in qadīr.

There is no god but Allāh: He is one and has no partners. For Him is the Dominion and all Praise, and He is capable of everything.

The deeds of the one who recites this will not be matched by anyone else in the world on a given day, save that the other person will have read the same.[25]

IV

Place your hand on your forehead and recite,

بِسْمِ اللهِ الَّذِىْ لَا اِلٰهَ اِلَّا هُوَ الرَّحْمٰنُ الرَّحِيْمُ
اَللّٰهُمَّ اَذْهِبْ عَنِّى الْهَمَّ وَ الْحُزْنَ

bismillāhi-l-ladhī lā ilāha illā huwa-r-raḥmānu-r-raḥīm. allāhumma adhhib 'anni-l-hamma wa-l-ḥuzn.

In the name of Allāh: there is no god but He, the Compassionate, the Most Merciful. O' Allāh! Remove me from grief and anxiety.[26]

This will protect from all anxiety and grief. This servant recites the following addition at the end,

وَ عَنْ اَهْلِ السُّنَّةِ

wa 'an ahli-s-sunnah.

And (remove grief and sorrow) from the *ahl al-sunnah.*

V

The five treasures of the Qādirī path:

After the *fajr* prayer:

يَا عَزِيْزُ يَا اَللّٰهُ   *yā ʿazīzu yā allāhu*   O' Majestic, O' Allāh!

After the *ẓuhr* prayer:

يَا كَرِيْمُ يَا اَللّٰهُ   *yā karīmu yā allāhu*   O' Generous, O' Allāh!

After the *ʿaṣr* prayer:

يَا جَبَّارُ يَا اَللّٰهُ   *yā jabbāru yā allāhu*   O' Powerful, O' Allāh!

After the *maghrib* prayer:

يَا سَتَّارُ يَا اَللّٰهُ   *yā sattāru yā allāhu*   O' Coverer, O' Allāh!

After the *ʿishāʾ* prayer:

يَا غَفَّارُ يَا اَللّٰهُ   *yā ghaffāru yā allāhu*   O' Forgiver, O' Allāh!

Recite one-hundred times each: this brings about innumerable blessings.

AFTER THE MORNING & AFTERNOON PRAYERS[i]

I

Without moving even a foot out of place (having finished the ritual prayer), recite:

لَا اِلٰهَ اِلَّا اللهُ وَحْدَهٗ لَا شَرِيْكَ لَهٗ وَلَهُ الْمُلْكُ وَلَهُ الْحَمْدُ بِيَدِهِ الْخَيْرُ يُحْيِيْ وَ يُمِيْتُ وَ هُوَ عَلٰى كُلِّ شَىْءٍ قَدِيْرٌ

lā ilāha illa-llāhu waḥdahū lā sharīka lah. wa lahu-l-mulku wa lahu-l-ḥamd. bi-yadihi-l-khayru yuḥyī wa yumīt. wa huwa ʻalā kulli shay'in qadīr.

There is no god but Allāh: He is one and has no partners. For him is the Dominion and all Praise. He controls all good. He gives life and death, and He is capable of everything.

Recite ten times for protection from every trial and tribulation, devil and disliked affair. One's sins will be forgiven and

---

i The morning prayer refers to *ṣalāt al-fajr* whilst the afternoon prayer refers to *ṣalāt al-ʻaṣr*.

no one's good deeds will compare to those of he who recites this.[27]

II

اَللّٰهُمَّ اَجِرْنِىْ مِنَ النَّارِ

allāhumma ajirnī mina-n-nār.

O' Allāh! Protect me from the Hellfire!

Recite seven times: Hellfire will supplicate, "O' Allāh! Save (the reciter) from me.".[28]

AFTER THE MORNING PRAYER

I

اَللّٰهُمَّ اكْفِنِىْ كُلَّ مُهِمٍّ مِّنْ حَيْثُ شِئْتَ وَ مِنْ
اَيْنَ شِئْتَ حَسْبِىَ اللّٰهُ لِدِيْنِىْ حَسْبِىَ اللّٰهُ لِدُنْيَاىَ
حَسْبِىَ اللّٰهُ لِمَآ اَهَمَّنِىْ حَسْبِىَ اللّٰهُ لِمَنْ بَغٰى
عَلَىَّ حَسْبِىَ اللّٰهُ لِمَنْ حسَدَنِىْ حَسْبِىَ اللّٰهُ لِمَنْ
كَادَنِىْ بِسُوْءٍ حَسْبِىَ اللّٰهُ عِنْدَ الْمَوْتِ حَسْبِىَ اللّٰهُ
عِنْدَ الْمَسْاَلَةِ فِى الْقَبْرِ حَسْبِىَ اللّٰهُ عِنْدَ الْمِيْزَانِ

حَسْبِيَ اللّٰهُ عِنْدَ الصِّرَاطِ حَسْبِيَ اللّٰهُ الَّذِىْ لَا اِلٰهَ اِلَّا هُوَ عَلَيْهِ تَوَكَّلْتُ وَ هُوَ رَبُّ الْعَرْشِ الْعَظِيْمِ

allāhumma-kfinī kulla muhimmi-m-min ḥaythu shi'ta wa min ayna shi'ta ḥasbiya-llāhu li-dīnī. ḥasbiya-llāhu li-dunyāy. ḥasbiya-llāhu li-mā ahammanī. ḥasbiya-llāhu li-mam baghā 'alayy. ḥasbiya-llāhu li-man ḥasadnī. ḥasbiya-llāhu li-man kādanī bi-sū'. ḥasbiya-llāhu 'inda-l-mawt. ḥasbiya-llāhu 'inda-l-mas'alati fi-l-qabr. ḥasbiya-llāhu 'inda-l-mīzān. ḥasbiya-llāhu 'inda-ṣ-ṣirāṭi. ḥasbiya-llāhu-l-ladhī lā ilāha illā hū. 'alayhi tawakkaltu wa huwa rabbu-l-'arshi-l-'aẓīm.

O' Allāh! Suffice me in every matter however and from wherever You will. Allāh suffices me in my religion. Allāh suffices me in my mortal life. Allāh suffices me in that which troubles me. Allāh suffices me in all who plot against me. Allāh suffices me for the one who envies me. Allāh suffices me for the one who intends to harm me. Allāh suffices me at the time of death. Allāh suffices me for the questions of the grave. Allāh suffices me at the time of the Scale. Allāh suffices me at the time of the Bridge. Allāh suffices me: there is no god but He. I trust in Him, and He is the Lord of the Almighty Throne.

By means of this recitation, every difficulty will be eased, all worries will be removed, one's faith will be protected, Allāh's assistance will remain in every situation, one's enemies will be destroyed, the envious one will be consumed by his own jealousy, the pangs of death will be eased, the grave will be spacious, one's good deeds will be weighty on the Scale and passage over the Bridge [*ṣirāṭ*] will be made easy.

II

Having performed the morning prayer, remain seated without moving even a foot out of place. Remain occupied in remembrance [*dhikr*] until the sun fully rises - meaning twenty to twenty-five minutes after sunrise. At this point, perform two units of ritual prayer [*ṣalāh*]: this is equivalent to the reward of a complete major and minor pilgrimage [*ḥajj wa 'umrah*].[29]

AFTER THE EVENING PRAYER[i]

Having read the obligatory [*farḍ*] units of ritual prayer [*ṣalāh*], read a further six with a single intention. Recite the testimony [*tashahhud*], prayers [*salām*] and supplication [*du'ā*] after every second unit and begin the first, third and fifth units with the opening supplication ("*subḥānaka-llāhumma...*"). The first two of these (units) will be the emphasised [*mu'akkadah*] sunnah, whilst the remainder will be voluntary [*nafl*]. Collectively, they form the prayer of *awwābīn*, and Allāh is forgiving to the one who performs this prayer.[30]

RECITE IN THE NIGHT (ANYTIME BETWEEN SUNSET AND DAWN)

I

Sūrat al-Mulk (Qur'ān, Chapter 67): for protection from the turmoils of the grave.[31]

II

Sūrah Yā-Sīn (Qur'ān, Chapter 36): for forgiveness.[32]

---

i The evening prayer refers to *ṣalāt al-maghrib.*

III

Sūrat al-Wāqiʿah (Qur'ān, Chapter 56): for protection from destitution.[33]

IV

Sūrat al-Dukhān (Qur'ān, Chapter 44): to rise the following morning with seventy thousand angels supplicating for one's forgiveness.[34]

AFTER THE NIGHTTIME PRAYER[i]

اَللّٰهُمَّ صَلِّ عَلٰى سَيِّدِنَا مُحَمَّدٍ كَمَا اَمَرْتَنَآ اَنْ
نُّصَلِّيَ عَلَيْهِ اَللّٰهُمَّ صَلِّ عَلٰى سَيِّدِنَا مُحَمَّدٍ كَمَا
هُوَ اَهْلُهٗ اَللّٰهُمَّ صَلِّ عَلٰى سَيِّدِنَا مُحَمَّدٍ كَمَا
تُحِبُّ وَتَرْضٰى لَهٗ اَللّٰهُمَّ صَلِّ عَلٰى رُوْحِ سَيِّدِنَا
مُحَمَّدٍ فِي الْاَرْوَاحِ اَللّٰهُمَّ صَلِّ عَلٰى جَسَدِ
سَيِّدِنَا مُحَمَّدٍ فِي الْاَجْسَادِ اَللّٰهُمَّ صَلِّ عَلٰى قَبْرِ
سَيِّدِنَا مُحَمَّدٍ فِي الْقُبُوْرِ صَلَّ اللهُ عَلٰى سَيِّدِنَا
وَمَولَانَا مُحَمَّدٍ

i The nighttime prayer refers to *ṣalāt al-ʿishā'*.

allāhumma ṣalli 'alā sayyidinā muḥammadin kamā amartanā an-n-nusalliya 'alayh. allāhumma ṣalli 'alā sayyidinā muḥammadin kamā huwa ahluh. allāhumma ṣalli 'alā sayyidinā muḥammadin kamā tuḥibbu wa tarḍā lah. allāhumma ṣalli 'alā rūḥi sayyidinā muḥammadin fi-l-arwāḥ. allāhumma ṣalli 'alā jasadi sayyidinā muḥammadin fi-l-ajsād. allāhumma ṣalli 'alā qabri sayyidinā muḥammadin fi-l-qubūr. ṣalla-llāhu 'alā sayyidinā muḥammad.

O' Allāh! Send prayers upon our master Muḥammad as You ordered us to invoke prayers upon him. O' Allāh! Send prayers upon our master Muḥammad as is his worth. O' Allāh! Send prayers upon our master Muḥammad as You are pleased and wish for him. O' Allāh! Send prayers upon the soul of our master Muḥammad amongst souls. O' Allāh! Send prayers upon the body of our master Muḥammad amongst bodies. O' Allāh! Send prayers upon the resting place of our master Muḥammad amongst graves.[35] Prayers of Allāh be upon our master and liege lord Muḥammad!

Recite this in an odd amount as much as one is able to regularly commit: there is no better phrasing than this to be blessed with the vision of the beloved Prophet ﷺ (in one's dreams). However, undertake this recitation with the soul intention of reverence for his blessed being, without assuming that you will be blessed with his vision: his generosity is without bounds or limits.

فراق و وصل چہ خواہی رضائے دوست طلب
کہ حیف باشد ازو غیرِ او تمنائے

Seperation or company, whichever you wish,
the friend's pleasure is all that is sought.
It would be oppression if you wished
for anything but this.

(Recite this) whilst facing the illuminated city of Madīnah with one's arms folded (as in the ritual prayer) and one's attention turned towards our noble master ﷺ. Imagine the resting place of the Prophet ﷺ to be present, and be certain that the Prophet ﷺ sees you, hears you and is aware of the flaws of your heart.

II

اَللّٰهُ لَآ اِلٰهَ اِلَّا هُوَ الْحَیُّ الْقَیُّوْمُ ط اَللّٰهُ لَآ اِلٰهَ اِلَّا

هُوَ الرَّحْمٰنُ الرَّحِيْمُ اَللّٰهُ لَا اِلٰهَ اِلَّا اَنْتَ سُبْحٰنَكَ
اِنِّيْ كُنْتُ مِنَ الظّٰلِمِيْنَ ط صَلِّ وَسَلِّمْ وَبَارِكْ اَبَدًا
عَلَى النَّبِيِّ الْاُمِّيِّ وَاٰلِهٖ وَاَصْحَابِهٖ اَجْمَعِيْنَ ط اَللّٰهُ
اللّٰهُ اَللّٰهُ لَا اِلٰهَ اِلَّا اللّٰهُ مُحَمَّدٌ رَّسُوْلُ اللّٰهِ صَلَّى
اللّٰهُ تَعَالٰى عَلَيْهِ وَسَلَّمَ يَا غَوْثُ يَا غَوْثُ يَا غَوْثُ

allāhu lā ilāha illā huwa-l-ḥayyu-l-qayyūm. allāhu lā ilāha illā huwa-r-raḥmānu-r-raḥīm. allāhu lā ilāha illā anta subḥānaka innī kuntu mina-ẓ-ẓālimīn. salli wa sallim wa bārik abadan 'ala-n-nabiyyi-l-ummiyy. wa ālihī wa asḥābihī ajma'īn. allāh. allāh. allāh. lā ilāha illa-llāhu muḥammadu-r-rasūlu-llāh. salla-llāhu ta'āla 'alayhi wa sallam. yā ghawth. yā ghawth. yā ghawth.

Allāh: there is no god but He: Ever-Living, Ever-Lasting. Allāh: there is no god but He: the Most Compassionate, the Merciful. Allāh: there is no god but You: glory be to You. Indeed, I have been of the wrongdoers. Send prayers and peace perpetually upon the primordial Prophet and his kinfolk and companions in their entirety! Allāh! Allāh! Allāh! There is no god but Allāh, and Muhammad ﷺ is the

Messenger of Allāh. O' Ghawth! O' Ghawth! O' Ghawth[i]!

Recite one hundred times for the forgiveness of one's sins and salvation from the tribulations of this world and the hereafter.

BEFORE SLEEPING

I

Recite the verse of the Throne [*āyat al-kursī*] (see Appendix 3) once: one will remain in Divine protection as long as they sleep. The house and the houses either side will be safe from thieves, black magic and evil spirits [*jinn*].[36]

II

Recite the litany [*tasbīḥ*] of Lady Fāṭimah ﷺ once (see page 27): one will wake refreshed in the morning alongside innumerable other benefits.[37]

III

Recite Sūrat al-Fātiḥah (see Appendix 1) and Sūrat

i 'Ghawth' refers to Shaykh 'Abd al-Qādir al-Jīlānī ﷺ.

al-Ikhlāṣ (see Appendix 6.1) once.[38]

IV

Recite the opening five and ending two verses of Sūrat al-Baqarah (see Appendix 2).

The aforementioned litanies (III and IV) bring about innumerable benefits.[39]

V

Recite the last four verses of Sūrat al-Kahf (see Appendix 4): one will awake the time they intend during the night or morning.[40]

VI

Spreading out both hands, recite the three '*qul*'-chapters (see Appendix 6) once each, then blow on one's hands and wipe over one's head, face, chest and entire body in every direction that one's hands can reach. Repeat this a second and third time: one will remain protected from every misfortune.[41]

VII

Recite Sūrat al-Kāfirūn (see Appendix 5) immediately

before sleeping. If one needs to speak after this, they should repeat this recitation after speaking: if Allāh wills, they will pass away upon this recitation.[42]

UPON RISING FROM SLEEP

اَلْحَمْدُ لِلّٰهِ الَّذِىْ اَحْيَانَا بَعْدَ مَآ اَمَا تَنَا وَاِلَيْهِ النُّشُوْرُ

al-ḥamdu li-llāhi-l-ladhī aḥyānā ba'da mā amātanā wa ilayhi-n-nushūr.

All praise is due to Allāh, who gave us life after giving us death, and to Him is our return.[43]

Recite once: if Allāh wills, one will also awake praising Allāh on the Day of Judgement.

NOTE: all of the litanies mentioned thus far should be commenced and concluded with invoking prayers and peace upon the Prophet ﷺ.

THE NIGHT VIGIL

If one sleeps for even a short period having read the obligatory units of the night prayer [*'ishā*] and then wakes before dawn - even if it is only early night, or even if in the winter they had read the night prayer at half-six in the evening and then fallen asleep to wake at seven-thirty - that is considered the time of the night vigil [*tahajjud*].

If one performs ablution [*wuḍū*] and offers a minimum of two units [*rak'āt*] of ritual prayer, that will be considered the night vigil. The Prophetic tradition narrates eight units of prayer[44] whilst the way of the Masters [*mashā'ikh*] is twelve units.

One is at liberty to recite what they wish, but it is preferable to recite whatever one has memorised of the Qur'ān in these units of prayer. If one has memorised the entire Qur'ān, they should complete an entire recitation in a minimum of three and a maximum of forty nights. If one has not memorised (a substantial portion of the Qur'ān), they can recite Sūrat al-Ikhlāṣ thrice in every unit and will receive the reward of reciting the entire Qur'ān in every unit of prayer.

THE REMEMBRANCE [DHIKR] OF THE FOUR STRIKES

Sit cross-legged with the saphenous vein of the left foot pressing into the innermost and second toe of the right foot. Lower one's head in the direction of the left knee and begin to vocalise the "l [*lām*]" of "*lā*" from here, stretching it whilst moving one's head parallel with the right knee.

Then begin to pronounce the "i [*hamzah*]" of "*ilāha*" and elongate the "a [*alif*]" that follows the "l [*lām*]" whilst raising the head to be parallel with the shoulders. Upon vocalising the "h [*hā'*]", vigorously turn one's gaze rightward before returning one's gaze as though to strike the heart whilst saying "*illa-llāhu*".

To begin, repeat this one-hundred times - or less, as one is able to manage - before increasing it as one's ability and time increases, ultimately aiming to perform five-thousand such "strikes" on the heart daily. When one's ardour begins to peak, recite,

مُحَمَّدٌ رَّسُوْلُ اللهِ صَلَّى اللهُ تَعَالٰى عَلَيْهِ وَعَلٰى
اٰلِهٖ وَاَصْحٰبِهٖ وَسَلَّمَ

muḥammadu-r-rasulu-llāh. ṣalla-llāhu ta'ālā 'alayhi wa 'alā ālihī wa aṣḥābihī wa sallam.

Three times after every one-hundred recitations, one will attain tranquillity. The novice will remain exclusively dependent on this ardour until the rust (of the heart) is expelled. Perform this remembrance in such a time and place where one will not become ostentatious, and where one will not disturb anyone praying, sleeping or recovering from illness. If one find's oneself becoming ostentatious, they should not abandon this remembrance but rather overpower their ostentation. Turn to Allāh ﷻ through the medium of the Prophet ﷺ and repent: if Allāh wills, one will be protected from ostentation and it will be overcome.

SILENT REMEMBRANCE

Sitting with one's legs folded (as in the ritual prayer), place one's tongue on the palate such that it doesn't move and utilise only one's imagination such that even one's breaths do not make a sound. One is free to adopt any of the following methods they wish or even adopt all of them from time to time.

(1) Lower one's head and begin vocalising the "*l* [*lām*]" of "*lā*" from the position of (one's gaze pointing towards) the naval. Raise one's head deliberately so as to reach the "*h* [*hā*]" of "*ilāha*" as one's gaze rises to the level of the mind. With this, vocalise the first "*i* [*hamzah*]" of

"*illa-llāhu*" from this position and thus strike towards the navel, as though upon the heart.

(2) In the same way, recite "*lā ilāha illā hū*", with "*illā hū*" replacing the second part (of the phrase).

(3) Recite only "*illa-llāhu*" by vocalising the first "*i* [*hamzah*]" from the navel, raising the head to vocalise "*illā-ll*" when one's head rises level to the mind and with this vocalise "*llāhu*" whilst lowering one's gaze to strike upon the navel or heart.

(4) Recite only "*Allāhu*" - beginning to vocalise the first "*a* [*hamzah*]" from the navel and raise one's head until "*lā*" before striking (the heart) whilst vocalising "*hu*".

(5) Recite only "*Allāh*" - without pronouncing a vowel on the "*h* [*hā'*]". Vocalise the first "*a* [*hamzah*]" whilst raising one's gaze from the navel, reaching "*l-* [*lām*]" level with one's mind and strike (the heart) upon "*-lāh*".

Begin this by completing one hundred repetitions, aiming to reach thousands of repetitions as one's ability and competence increases. The most virtuous of these five (methods) is the first. This method is so beneficial that they are generally concealed and transmitted only in purisms, yet this servant has made them public for the brethren of the path [*ṭarīqah*].

(REMEMBRANCE OF) INHALATION & EXHALATION

Maintain this remembrance [*dhikr*] with every inhalation and exhalation - using means of any of the five aforementioned phrasings - whether one is standing, seated, walking, in or out of the state of ablution - even when one is attending the call of nature. When one reaches a stage where this action no longer requires conscious effort, every breath they take - even whilst sleeping - will be occupied in this remembrance.

ENVISAGING ONE'S GUIDE [TAṢAWWUR AL-SHAYKH]

In a secluded place far from all distractions, sit facing the home of one's guide or his grave if he has passed away. In perfect silence, envisage the form of one's guide, imagining one's self to be present before him. Envisage that Prophetic auroras and blessings are infusing the heart of one's guide, and that one's own heart is below the heart of the guide in a state of destitute beseeching. Imagine these auroras and blessings to be cascading from the heart of the guide and inculcating one's own heart.

Maintain this practice until it becomes enduring and no longer requires conscious effort. Eventually, this form of the guide will become quintessential and remain with the aspirant at all times, assisting them in every task and informing them of the solution to every obstacle in their path.

NOTE: before occupying one's self in the performance of litanies and spiritual exercises, one should perform any missed prayers or fasts they may have to the best of their abilities. The recommended [*mustaḥabb*] deeds of the one who has outstanding obligations do not benefit him, and indeed are not accepted until he completes his missed obligations.

The effectiveness of litanies and spiritual exercises is predicated upon three things: (1) limiting one's food intake, (2) limiting one's conversation, and (3) limiting one's sleep. And with Allāh is enabling grace [*tawfīq*]!

The destitute servant,
Aḥmad Riḍā Qādirī,
may Allāh forgive him.

5 Muḥarram al-Ḥarām 1338 AH.

APPENDIX 1

SŪRAT AL-FĀTIHAH (QUR'ĀN, CHAPTER 1)

بِسۡمِ ٱللَّهِ ٱلرَّحۡمَٰنِ ٱلرَّحِيمِ ١

ٱلۡحَمۡدُ لِلَّهِ رَبِّ ٱلۡعَٰلَمِينَ ٢ ٱلرَّحۡمَٰنِ ٱلرَّحِيمِ
٣ مَٰلِكِ يَوۡمِ ٱلدِّينِ ٤ إِيَّاكَ نَعۡبُدُ وَإِيَّاكَ
نَسۡتَعِينُ ٥ ٱهۡدِنَا ٱلصِّرَٰطَ ٱلۡمُسۡتَقِيمَ ٦
صِرَٰطَ ٱلَّذِينَ أَنۡعَمۡتَ عَلَيۡهِمۡ غَيۡرِ ٱلۡمَغۡضُوبِ
عَلَيۡهِمۡ وَلَا ٱلضَّآلِّينَ ٧

bismillāhi-r-raḥmāni-r-raḥīm. al-ḥamdu li-lāhi-r-rabbi-l-'ālamīn. a-r-raḥmāni-r-raḥīm. māliki yawmi-d-dīn. iyyāka n'abudu wa iyyāka nasta'īn. ihdina-ṣ-ṣirāṭa-l-mustaqīm. ṣirāṭa-l-ladhīna an'amta 'alayhim ghayri-l-maghḍūbi 'alayhim wa la-ḍ-ḍāllīn.

Allāh's name I begin with: the Most Compassionate, the Most Merciful. All praise belongs to Allāh, the Lord of all the worlds.

The Most Compassionate, the Most Merciful. Master of the Day of Recompense. You alone we worship, You alone we ask for help. Guide us on the straight path: the path of those You have favoured, not of those who have incurred anger, nor who have gone astray.

APPENDIX 2

1 – FIRST FIVE VERSES OF SŪRAT AL-BAQARAH (QUR'ĀN, CHAPTER 2, V. 1-5)

بِسْمِ ٱللَّهِ ٱلرَّحْمَـٰنِ ٱلرَّحِيمِ

الٓمٓ ١ ذَٰلِكَ ٱلْكِتَـٰبُ لَا رَيْبَ ۛ فِيهِ ۛ هُدًى
لِّلْمُتَّقِينَ ٢ ٱلَّذِينَ يُؤْمِنُونَ بِٱلْغَيْبِ وَيُقِيمُونَ
ٱلصَّلَوٰةَ وَمِمَّا رَزَقْنَـٰهُمْ يُنفِقُونَ ٣ وَٱلَّذِينَ
يُؤْمِنُونَ بِمَآ أُنزِلَ إِلَيْكَ وَمَآ أُنزِلَ مِن قَبْلِكَ
وَبِٱلْـَٔاخِرَةِ هُمْ يُوقِنُونَ ٤ أُو۟لَـٰٓئِكَ عَلَىٰ هُدًى
مِّن رَّبِّهِمْ ۖ وَأُو۟لَـٰٓئِكَ هُمُ ٱلْمُفْلِحُونَ ٥

alif-lām-mīm. dhālika-l-kitābu lā rayba fīhi huda-l-li-l-muttaqīn. al-ladhīna yu'minūna bi-l-ghaybi wa yuqīmūna-ṣ-ṣalāta wa mimmā razaqnāhum yunfiqūn. wa-l-ladhīna yu'minūna bi-mā unzila ilayka wa mā unzila min qablika wa bi-l-ākhirati hum yūqinūn. ūlā'ika 'alā huda-m-mi-r-rabbihim wa ūlā'ika humu-l-mufliḥūn.

Alif, lām, mīm. That lofty scripture in which there is no scope for doubt, containing guidance for those who fear (Allāh), who believe without seeing, maintain the prayer, and give (in Our way) of what We have provided for them. Those who believe in that which was revealed to you (O' Beloved Prophet), and in what was revealed before you, those who have certainty in the Hereafter. They alone are following guidance from their Lord, and they alone will prosper.

2 – LAST TWO VERSES OF SŪRAT AL-BAQARAH (QUR'ĀN, CHAPTER 2, V. 285-286)

ءَامَنَ ٱلرَّسُولُ بِمَآ أُنزِلَ إِلَيۡهِ مِن رَّبِّهِۦ
وَٱلۡمُؤۡمِنُونَۚ كُلٌّ ءَامَنَ بِٱللَّهِ وَمَلَـٰٓئِكَتِهِۦ وَكُتُبِهِۦ
وَرُسُلِهِۦ لَا نُفَرِّقُ بَيۡنَ أَحَدٖ مِّن رُّسُلِهِۦۚ وَقَالُواْ
سَمِعۡنَا وَأَطَعۡنَاۖ غُفۡرَانَكَ رَبَّنَا وَإِلَيۡكَ ٱلۡمَصِيرُ
﴿٢٨٥﴾ لَا يُكَلِّفُ ٱللَّهُ نَفۡسًا إِلَّا وُسۡعَهَاۚ لَهَا

مَا كَسَبَتْ وَعَلَيْهَا مَا ٱكْتَسَبَتْ ۗ رَبَّنَا لَا تُؤَاخِذْنَآ إِن نَّسِينَآ أَوْ أَخْطَأْنَا ۚ رَبَّنَا وَلَا تَحْمِلْ عَلَيْنَآ إِصْرًا كَمَا حَمَلْتَهُۥ عَلَى ٱلَّذِينَ مِن قَبْلِنَا ۚ رَبَّنَا وَلَا تُحَمِّلْنَا مَا لَا طَاقَةَ لَنَا بِهِۦ ۖ وَٱعْفُ عَنَّا وَٱغْفِرْ لَنَا وَٱرْحَمْنَآ ۚ أَنتَ مَوْلَىٰنَا فَٱنصُرْنَا عَلَى ٱلْقَوْمِ ٱلْكَٰفِرِينَ ﴿٢٨٦﴾

āmana-r-rasūlu bimā unzila ilayhi mi-r-rabbihī wa-l-mu'minūn. kullun āmana bi-llāhi wa malā'ikatihī wa kutubihī wa rusulih. lā nufarriqu bayna aḥadi-m-mi-r-rusulih. wa qālū' sami'nā wa aṭa'nā ghufrānaka rabbanā wa ilayka-l-maṣīr. lā yukallifu-llāhu nafsan illā wus'ahā lahā mā kasabat wa 'alayhā ma-ktasabat. rabbanā lā tu'ākhidhnā in-nasīnā aw akhṭa'nā. rabbanā wa lā taḥmil 'alaynā iṣran kamā ḥamaltahū 'ala-l-ladhīna min qablinā rabbanā wa lā tuḥammilnā mā lā ṭāqata lanā bih. wa-'fu 'annā wa-ghfir lanā wa-raḥmnā anta mawlānā fa-nṣurnā 'ala-l-qawmi-l-kāfirīn.

The Messenger believes in what has been sent down to him from his Lord, as do the believers. They all believe in Allāh, His angels, His scriptures, and His messengers, saying, "We make no distinction between (believing in) any of His messengers." And they say, "We have heard and obeyed; (grant us) Your forgiveness, our Lord - to You alone is the return. Allāh does not burden any soul except with that which it can bear: each gains whatever good it has earned, and suffers whatever evil it has earned - "Our Lord, do not condemn us if we forget or are mistaken. Our Lord, do not heavily burden us as You burdened those before us. Our Lord, do not burden us with a burden we cannot bear. Pardon us, forgive us, and have mercy on us. You are our Protector, so assist us against the disbelievers."

APPENDIX 3

THE VERSE OF THE THRONE [ĀYAT AL-KURSĪ] (QUR'ĀN, CHAPTER 2, V. 255)

اللَّهُ لَا إِلَٰهَ إِلَّا هُوَ الْحَيُّ الْقَيُّومُ ۚ لَا تَأْخُذُهُ سِنَةٌ
وَلَا نَوْمٌ ۚ لَّهُ مَا فِي السَّمَاوَاتِ وَمَا فِي الْأَرْضِ ۗ
مَن ذَا الَّذِي يَشْفَعُ عِندَهُ إِلَّا بِإِذْنِهِ ۚ يَعْلَمُ
مَا بَيْنَ أَيْدِيهِمْ وَمَا خَلْفَهُمْ ۖ وَلَا يُحِيطُونَ

بِشَيْءٍ مِّنْ عِلْمِهِ إِلَّا بِمَا شَاءَ ۚ وَسِعَ كُرْسِيُّهُ السَّمَاوَاتِ وَالْأَرْضَ ۖ وَلَا يَئُودُهُ حِفْظُهُمَا ۚ وَهُوَ الْعَلِيُّ الْعَظِيمُ

allāhu lā ilāha illā huwa-l-ḥayyu-l-qayyūm. lā ta'khudhuhū sinatu-w-wa lā nawm. lahū mā fi-samāwāti wa mā fi-l-arḍ. man dha-la-dhī yashfa'u 'indahū illā bi-idhnih. ya'lamu mā bayna aydīhim wa mā khalfahum. wa lā yuḥīṭūna bi-shay'i-m-min 'ilmihī illā bi-mā shā'. wasi'a kursiyyuhu-s-samāwāti wa-l-arḍ. wa lā ya'ūduhu ḥifẓuhumā wa huwwa-l-'aliyyu-l-'aẓīm.

Allāh: there is no god but Him, the Ever Living, the Ever Watchful. Neither slumber nor sleep overtakes Him. All that is in the heavens and in the earth belongs to Him. Who is there that can intercede with Him except by His leave? He knows what is before them and what is behind them, but they do not comprehend any of His knowledge except what He wills. His throne extends over the heavens and the earth; it does not weary Him to preserve them both. He is the Most High, the Tremendous.

APPENDIX 4

LAST FOUR VERSES OF SŪRAT AL-KAHF
(QUR'ĀN, CHAPTER 18, V. 107-110)

إِنَّ ٱلَّذِينَ ءَامَنُواْ وَعَمِلُواْ ٱلصَّٰلِحَٰتِ كَانَتۡ
لَهُمۡ جَنَّٰتُ ٱلۡفِرۡدَوۡسِ نُزُلًا ﴿١٠٧﴾ خَٰلِدِينَ فِيهَا
لَا يَبۡغُونَ عَنۡهَا حِوَلٗا ﴿١٠٨﴾ قُل لَّوۡ كَانَ ٱلۡبَحۡرُ
مِدَادٗا لِّكَلِمَٰتِ رَبِّي لَنَفِدَ ٱلۡبَحۡرُ قَبۡلَ أَن
تَنفَدَ كَلِمَٰتُ رَبِّي وَلَوۡ جِئۡنَا بِمِثۡلِهِۦ مَدَدٗا
﴿١٠٩﴾ قُلۡ إِنَّمَآ أَنَا۠ بَشَرٞ مِّثۡلُكُمۡ يُوحَىٰٓ إِلَيَّ
أَنَّمَآ إِلَٰهُكُمۡ إِلَٰهٞ وَٰحِدٞۖ فَمَن كَانَ يَرۡجُواْ
لِقَآءَ رَبِّهِۦ فَلۡيَعۡمَلۡ عَمَلٗا صَٰلِحٗا وَلَا يُشۡرِكۡ
بِعِبَادَةِ رَبِّهِۦٓ أَحَدَۢا ﴿١١٠﴾

inna-l-ladhīna āmanū' wa 'amilu-ṣ-ṣāliḥāti kānat lahum jannātu-l-firdawsi nuzulā. khālidīna fīhā lā yabghūna 'anhā ḥiwalā. qul-law kāna-l-baḥru midāda-l-likalimāti rabbī lanafida-l-baḥru qabla an tanfada kalimātu rabbī wa law ji'nā bi-mithlihī madadā. qul innamā ana basharu-m-mithlukum yūḥā ilayya annamā ilāhukum ilāhu-w-wāḥid. faman kāna yarjū' liqā'a rabbihī fa-l-ya'mal 'amalan ṣāliḥa-w-wa lā yushrik bi-'ibādati rabbihī aḥadā.

Indeed, those who believed and did good deeds, theirs are the Gardens of Paradise as a welcome. There they will forever remain, never wishing to leave. Say, "if the ocean were ink for the words of my Lord, it would surely be depleted and the words of my Lord would never be exhausted, even if We brought another (ocean) like it to assist." Say, "I am (physically) a human like you, to whom it is revealed that your God is only One God. Whoever hopes to meet his Lord should do good deeds and admit no one as a partner in the worship of his Lord."

APPENDIX 5

SŪRAT AL-KĀFIRŪN
(QUR'ĀN, CHAPTER 109)

بِسْمِ ٱللَّهِ ٱلرَّحْمَٰنِ ٱلرَّحِيمِ

قُلْ يَٰٓأَيُّهَا ٱلْكَٰفِرُونَ ١ لَآ أَعْبُدُ مَا تَعْبُدُونَ
٢ وَلَآ أَنتُمْ عَٰبِدُونَ مَآ أَعْبُدُ ٣ وَلَآ أَنَا۠ عَابِدٌ

مَّا عَبَدتُّمْ ۝٤ وَلَآ أَنتُمْ عَٰبِدُونَ مَآ أَعْبُدُ ۝٥
لَكُمْ دِينُكُمْ وَلِىَ دِينِ ۝٦

qul yā ayyuha-l-kāfirūn. lā a'budhu mā ta'budūn. wa lā antum 'ābidūna mā a'bud. wa lā ana 'ābidu-m-mā 'aba-t-tum. wa lā antum 'ābidūna mā a'bud. lakum dīnukum wa liya dīn.

Say, "O' Disbelievers: I do not worship what you worship, nor you worship what I worship. Nor will I worship what you worship, nor will you worship what I worship: you have your religion and I have my religion."

APPENDIX 6

1 – SŪRAT AL-IKHLĀṢ (QUR'ĀN, CHAPTER 112)

بِسْمِ ٱللَّهِ ٱلرَّحْمَٰنِ ٱلرَّحِيمِ

قُلْ هُوَ ٱللَّهُ أَحَدٌ ۝١ ٱللَّهُ ٱلصَّمَدُ ۝٢ لَمْ يَلِدْ
وَلَمْ يُولَدْ ۝٣ وَلَمْ يَكُن لَّهُۥ كُفُوًا أَحَدٌۢ ۝٤

qul huwa-llāhu aḥad. allāhu-ṣ-ṣamad. lam yalid wa lam yūlad. wa lam yaku-l-lahū kufuwan aḥad.

Say: Allāh is One. Allāh is the Self-Sufficient Sustainer. He is neither born nor gives birth. And there is none like Him.

2 – SŪRAT AL-FALAQ (QUR'ĀN, CHAPTER 113)

بِسۡمِ ٱللَّهِ ٱلرَّحۡمَٰنِ ٱلرَّحِيمِ

قُلۡ أَعُوذُ بِرَبِّ ٱلۡفَلَقِ ١ مِن شَرِّ مَا خَلَقَ ٢
وَمِن شَرِّ غَاسِقٍ إِذَا وَقَبَ ٣ وَمِن شَرِّ ٱلنَّفَّٰثَٰتِ
فِي ٱلۡعُقَدِ ٤ وَمِن شَرِّ حَاسِدٍ إِذَا حَسَدَ ٥

qul a'ūdhu bi-rabbi-l-falaq. min sharri mā khalaq. wa min sharri ghāsiqin idhā waqab. wa min sharri-n-naffāththāti fi-l-'uqad. wa min sharri ḥāsidin idhā ḥasad.

Say, "I take refuge with the Lord who creates the daybreak against the evil of all He has created, the evil of darkness when it falls, the evil of witches when they blow on knots, and the harm of the envier when he envies me."

3- SŪRAT AL-NĀS
(QUR'ĀN, CHAPTER 114)

بِسْمِ ٱللَّهِ ٱلرَّحْمَٰنِ ٱلرَّحِيمِ

قُلْ أَعُوذُ بِرَبِّ ٱلنَّاسِ ۝١ مَلِكِ ٱلنَّاسِ ۝٢ إِلَٰهِ
ٱلنَّاسِ ۝٣ مِن شَرِّ ٱلْوَسْوَاسِ ٱلْخَنَّاسِ ۝٤ ٱلَّذِى
يُوَسْوِسُ فِى صُدُورِ ٱلنَّاسِ ۝٥ مِنَ ٱلْجِنَّةِ وَٱلنَّاسِ ۝٦

qul a'ūdhu bi-rabbi-n-nās. maliki-n-nās. ilāhi-n-nās. min sharri-l-waswāsi-l-khannās. al-ladhī yuwaswisu fī ṣudūri-n-nās. mina-l-jinnati wa-n-nās.

Say, "I take refuge with the Lord of all people, the King of all people, the God of all people, against the evil of the hidden whisperer (of evil thoughts) - who whispers into the hearts of people - *jinn* and human."

REFERENCES

1. *Qur'ān*, 40/1-3.
2. *Sunan abī dawūd*, vol. 4, p. 414, *ḥadīth* 5057 & 5082. *Sunan al-tirmidhī*, vol. 4, p. 402, *ḥadīth* 2888.
3. *Al-durr al-manthūr*, vol. 5, p. 434.
4. *Sunan al-tirmidhī*, vol. 5, p. 346, *ḥadīth* 3616.
5. *Sunan abī dawūd*, vol. 4, p. 418, *ḥadīth* 5088.
6. *Al-muṣannaf li ibn abī shaybah*, vol. 7, p. 41, *ḥadīth* 8.
7. *Al-durr al-manthūr*, vol. 4, p. 432.
8. *Al-durr al-manthūr*, vol. 6, p. 489.
9. *Qur'ān*, 23/115-118.
10. *Sunan al-tirmidhī*, vol. 4, p. 146, *ḥadīth* 2931.
11. *Al-musnad li-imām aḥmad b. ḥanbal*, vol. 9, p. 146, *ḥadīth* 19625.
12. *Fayḍ al-qadīr sharḥ al-jāmi' al-ṣaghīr*, vol. 4, p. 683, *ḥadīth* 6139 & 6140.
13. *Shu'b al-īmān li-l-bayhaqī*, vol. 4, p. 89, *ḥadīth* 4368.
14. *Firdaws al-akhbār li-l-daylamī*, vol. 2, p. 316, *ḥadīth* 7459.
15. *Sunan abī dawūd*, vol. 4, p. 412, *ḥadīth* 5069.
16. *Al-mu'jam al-awsaṭ li-l-ṭabrānī*, vol. 4, p. 152, *ḥadīth* 5538.
17. *Sunan abī dawūd*, vol. 2, p. 133, *ḥadīth* 1555.

18. *Kashf al-khufā'*, vol. 1, p. 352, *ḥadīth* 1274.

19. *Sunan al-kubrā li-l-nisā'ī*, vol. 6, p. 150, *ḥadīth* 10417.

20. *Ḥilyat al-awliyā'*, vol. 8, p. 309, *ḥadīth* 12312.

21. *Al-durr al-manthūr*, vol. 8, p. 681.

22. *Al-musnad li-imām aḥmad b. ḥanbal*, vol. 7, p. 357, *ḥadīth* 20625.

23. *Mishkāt al-maṣābīḥ*, vol. 1, p. 197, *ḥadīth* 974.

24. *Sunan al-tirmidhī*, vol. 5, p. 336, *ḥadīth* 3588.

25. *Al-iḥsān bi-tartīb ṣaḥīḥ ibn ḥibbān*, vol. 3, p. 231, *ḥadīth* 2012.

26. *Majma' al-zawā'id*, vol. 10, p. 144, *ḥadīth* 16971.

27. *Al-musnad li-imām aḥmad b. ḥanbal*, vol. 6, p. 289, *ḥadīth* 18012.

28. *Musnad abī ya'lā*, vol. 5, p. 289, *ḥadīth* 18012.

29. *Sunan al-tirmidhī*, vol. 2, p. 100, *ḥadīth* 586.

30. *Al-durr al-mukhtār wa radd al-muḥtār*, vol. 2, p.

547. *Al-mu'jam al-awsaṭ li-l-ṭabrānī*, vol. 5, p. 255, *ḥadīth* 7245.

31. *Sunan al-tirmidhī*, vol. 4, p. 407, *ḥadīth* 2899.

32. *Shu'b al-īmān li-l-bayhaqī*, vol. 2, p. 479, *ḥadīth* 2458.

33. *Shu'b al-īmān li-l-bayhaqī*, vol. 2, p. 491, *ḥadīth* 2497.

34. *Sunan al-tirmidhī*, vol. 4, p. 406, *ḥadīth* 2897.

35. *Sa'ādat al-dārayn*, p. 444.

36. *Shu'b al-īmān li-l-bayhaqī*, vol. 2, p. 458, *ḥadīth* 2395.
37. *Ṣaḥīḥ muslim*, p. 1460, *ḥadīth* 2728.
38. *Al-jāmi' al-ṣaghīr li-l-Suyūṭī*, p. 61, *ḥadīth* 892.
39. *Ṣaḥīḥ al-bukhārī*, vol. 3, p. 405, *ḥadīth* 5009. *Shu'b al-īmān li-l-bayhaqī*, vol. 2, p. 464, *ḥadīth* 2412.
40. *Sunan al-dāramī*, vol. 2, p. 546, *ḥadīth* 3406.
41. *Ṣaḥīḥ al-bukhārī*, vol. 3, p. 407, *ḥadīth* 5017. *Tafsīr rūḥ al-bayān*, vol. 4, p. 295.
42. *Al-jāmi' al-ṣaghīr li-l-suyūṭī*, p. 28, *ḥadīth* 367.
43. *Ṣaḥīḥ al-bukhārī*, vol. 4, p. 192, *ḥadīth* 6312.
44. *Radd al-muḥtār*, vol. 2, p. 566-567.

BIBLIOGRAPHY

Aṣbahānī, Abū Na'īm Aḥmad b. 'Abd-Allāh al-. *Ḥilyat al-awliyā'*. Beirut: Dar Al Kotob Al Ilmiyah, 1998.

Bakr, Nūr al-Dīn 'Alī b. Abī. *Majma' al-zawā'id*. Beirut: Dār al-Fikr, 2000.

Barūswī, Ismā'īl Ḥaqqī b. Muṣṭafā al-. *Tafsīr rūḥ al-bayān*. N.p., n.d.

Bayhaqī, Abū Bakr Aḥmad b. al-Ḥusayn al-. *Shu'b al-īmān*. Beirut: Dar Al Kotob Al Ilmiyah, 2001.

Bukhārī, Muḥammad b. Ismā'īl al-. *Ṣaḥīḥ al-bukhārī*. Beirut: Dar Al Kotob Al Ilmiyah, 1999.

Dāramī, 'Abd-Allāh b. 'Abd al-Raḥmān al-. *Sunan al-dāramī*. Dār al-Fikr, 1987.

Daylamī, Abu Shujā' Shīrawyah b. Shahardār al-. *Firdaws al-akhbār*. Beirut: Dār al-Fikr, 1986.

Daynūrī, Abū Bakr Aḥmad b. Muḥammad al-. *'Amal al-yawm wa al-laylah*. City: Dār al-Kitāb al-'Arabī, 1998.

Fārsī, Amīr 'Alā' al-Dīn b. Balbān. *Al-iḥsān bi-tartīb ṣaḥīḥ ibn ḥibbān*. Beirut: Dar Al Kotob Al Ilmiyah, n.d.

Ḥanbal, Aḥmad b.. *Al-musnad*. Beirut: Dār al-Fikr, 1994.

Ḥaṣkafī, 'Alā' al-Dīn Muḥammad b. 'Alī al-. *Al-durr*

al-mukhtār. Beirut: Dār al-Ma'rifah, n.d.

Jurāfī, Ismā'īl b. Muḥammad al-. *Kashf al-khufā'*. Beirut: Dar Al Kotob Al Ilmiyah, 2002

Khān, Aḥmad Riḍā. *Kanz al-īmān fī tarjamat al-qur'ān*. Karachi: Maktaba Tul Madina, 2012.

---. *Al-waẓīfat al-karīmah*. Karachi: Maktaba Tul Madina, 2010.

Khān, Muṣṭafā Riḍā. *Al-malfūẓ al-sharīf*. Karachi: Maktaba Tul Madinah, 2011.

Kūfī, 'Abd-Allāh b. Muḥammad Abi Shaybah al-. *Al-muṣannaf*. Beirut: Dār al-Fikr, 1994.

Mājah, Muḥammad b. Yazīd b.. *Sunan ibn majāh*. Beirut: Dār al-Ma'rifah, 2000.

Manāwī, Muḥammad 'Abd al-Rā'ūf al-. *Fayḍ al-qadīr*. Beirut: Dar Al Kotob Al Ilmiyah, 2012.

Mawṣalī, Abū Ya'lā Aḥmad b. 'Alī al-. *Al-musnad*. Beirut: Dar Al Kotob Al Ilmiyah, 1998.

Nabahānī, Yūsuf b. Ismā'īl al-. *Sa'ādat al-dārayn*. Beirut: Dar Al Kotob Al Ilmiyah, 2012.

Nisā'ī, Abū 'Abd al-Raḥmān Aḥmad al-. *Al-sunan al-kubrā*. Beirut: Dar Al Kotob Al Ilmiyah, 1991.

Nīshapūrī, Muḥammad b. 'Abd-Allāh al-Ḥākim al-. *Al-mustadrak*. Beirut: Dār al-Ma'rifah, 1998.

Qushayrī, Muslim b. al-Ḥajjāj al-. *Ṣaḥīḥ muslim*. Beirut: Dār Ibn Hazm, 1999.

Sijistānī, Abū Dāwūd Sulaymān al-. *Sunan abī dāwūd*.

Beirut: Dār al-Fikr, 2001.
Shāmī, Ibn 'Ābidīn al-. *Radd al-muḥtār*. Beirut: Dār al-Ma'rifah, n.d.
Suyūṭī, Jalāl al-Dīn al-. *Al-durr al-manthūr*. Beirut: Dār al-Fikr, 1983.
---. *Al-jāmi' al-ṣaghīr*. Beirut: Dar Al Kotob Al Ilmiyah, 2016.
Ṭabrānī, Sulaymān b. Aḥmad al-. *Al-mu'jam al-awsaṭ*. City: Dār Ihyā' Turāth al-'Arabī, 2000.
Tabrayzī, Muḥammad b. 'Abd-Allāh al-Khaṭīb al-. *Mishkāt al-maṣābīḥ*. Beirut: Dar Al Kotob Al Ilmiyah, 2003.
---. *Al-mu'jam al-kabīr*. City: Dār Ihyā' Turāth al-'Arabī, 2002.
Tirmidhī, Muḥammad b. 'Īsā al-. *Jāmi' al-tirmidhī*. Beirut: Dār al-Fikr, 1994.

NOTE: The names of Arabic and Urdu publishers have not been transliterated if they publicise an English spelling of their name, enabling the reader to easily search for their publications and contact details. Similarly, the titles of Arabic and Urdu works have only been transliterated if the publishers have not published an English spelling of the title.

www.ingramcontent.com/pod-product-compliance
Lightning Source LLC
Chambersburg PA
CBHW030531080526
44586CB00011B/397
* 9 7 8 1 9 9 9 7 7 2 0 1 7 *